Introduction to United States Culture

Eric J. Miller

Introduction to United States Culture

For requests or inquiries, please contact the author at: ejmjapan@gmail.com

Author: Eric J. Miller
Cover design: Andrew Thompson

Photo/Image credits:
Cover: small American flags by Lipton Sale; Inside cover: 1972 Schwinn Stingray by David Miller; Unit 1: relief location map of the USA 2010, image by Uwe Dedering; Unit 2: 1777 "Betsy Ross flag" image by Devin Cook; Map of present-day USA with the thirteen original colonies highlighted by Connormah; Unit 3: Times Square at night 2013 by Chensiyuan; Unit 4: State Seal of Alaska and State Seal of Hawaii; Unit 5: Voyages of Christopher Columbus by viajes_de_colon; Unit 6: Sioux chiefs by Edward S. Curtis circa 1905, Library of Congress; Unit 7: *The First Fight for Independence, Lexington Common, April 19, 1775* by William Barnes Wollen; Unit 8: Abraham Lincoln by Alexander Gardner 1863; Unit 9: *Buffalo Bill's Wild West and congress of rough riders of the world* circa 1899, Library of Congress; United States territorial acquisitions mid-century from the National Atlas of the United States; Unit 10: Astronaut Buzz Aldrin walks on the moon 1969, official NASA photograph; Unit 11: Staff of President Clinton's One America Initiative 1998 by White House photographer; Unit 12: United States Capitol west side 2013 by Martin Falbisoner; Unit 13: Martin Luther King 1964 by Nobel Foundation; Unit 14: 1910 Model T Ford by Harry Shipler; Unit 15: Hollywood Sign in Los Angeles, California by Thomas Wolf; Unit 16: Sliders and French fries by Jeffrey W; Unit 17: Grand Canyon, photo by John Kees; Unit 18: Steve Jobs and Bill Gates, 31 May 2007 by Joi Ito; Unit 19: Christmas tree at Rockefeller Plaza, New York by Alsandro; Unit 20: WTC in February 2016 by JJ Bers.

ISBN-13: 978-1530715725
ISBN-10: 1530715725

An **Answer Key** for the questions in this book is available free of charge in PDF format for schools/instructors who have purchased this book for use in their classes.
Please contact the author at ejmjapan@gmail.com to request this file.

Introduction to United States Culture

Table of Contents .... Page

Introduction: What is culture?

What is culture? It's a difficult question to answer.

According to the *Merriam-Webster* dictionary, **culture** is …
1) the beliefs, customs, arts, etc., of a particular society or group,
2) a particular society that has its own beliefs, ways of life, art, etc.,
3) a way of thinking, behaving, or working that exists in a place or group.

Another good way to think of culture is as a shared set of experiences among a group of people in a certain place or time. In other words, all of the things that you have experienced—the way your family lives, the schools you attended and the things you learned there, the holidays you celebrate, the foods you eat, the clothes you wear, how you greet other people, etc.—may be very similar to the other people around you. Sharing those things is what makes up your culture.

In some countries, most of the people share the same experiences. Japan is an example of a country said to have a "homogeneous" culture. In general, it is made up of the same kind of people who have similar experiences. As a result, we can say with more certainty what "Japanese culture" is.

The United States, on the other hand, is said to be a "diverse" country. In other words, there are many different kinds of Americans who sometimes have quite different experiences. For example, a group of young, black Americans living in New York City has probably had very different experiences than a group of older, white Americans living in North Dakota. So, it is sometimes difficult to say exactly what "American culture" is. Not all Americans have shared the same lifestyle, education, holidays, food, or even language. And today, perhaps, more than ever, the USA is a diverse country, made up of people of different races, religions, and political beliefs. Keep that in mind as you read this book.

Unit 1: From Sea to Shining Sea

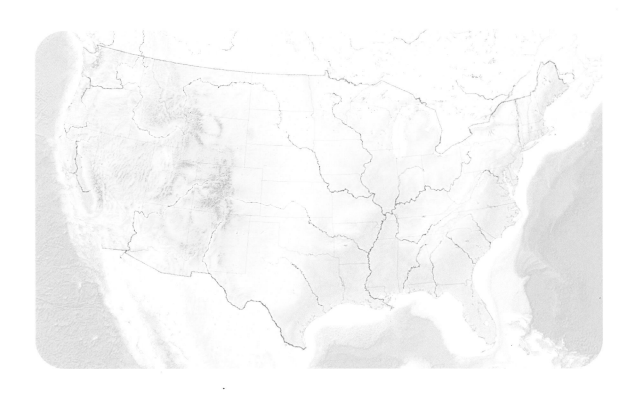

Warm Up

1. Have you ever been to another country? Where did you go?

2. How big is the USA compared to your country?

3. How many US states can you name?

Reading

From Sea to Shining Sea

The United States of America is a big country—the third largest country in the world. The part of the USA you see in the picture is sometimes called "the continental USA" or "the Lower 48" because it is made up of 48 states that cover the continent of North America. The two states you don't see in the picture are Alaska and Hawaii. The continental USA stretches from the Atlantic Ocean on the East Coast to the Pacific Ocean on the West Coast. Canada is located to the north of the USA, and Mexico is located to the southwest.

The size of each state in the USA is quite different. Alaska is the biggest state. In fact, there are fewer than 20 countries in the world that are bigger than Alaska. Rhode Island is the smallest state—it is about 500 times smaller than Alaska. But, Rhode Island has more people than Alaska. The state with the highest population is California. There are a lot of people in the USA—about 320 million—but the population density of the USA is much lower than other developed countries like Japan, England, and Germany.

You can find almost every type of geography and climate in the USA. Some states are warm and dry, like Arizona. Other states are very cold in winter, such as Minnesota. Some states are flat with wide open spaces, like Kansas. Other states are covered with mountains, such as Colorado. Most states have four seasons, but temperatures in summer and winter vary greatly from state to state.

The names of the states are also interesting. Many states have names that come from Native American languages. Other states were given their names by the Europeans who settled there. Only one state is named after an American person—Washington.

Quiz
Choose the best answer for each question.

1. How many states are there in the USA?
   A. 13   C. 50
   B. 48   D. 500

2. Which state in the USA has the most people?
   A. Alaska   C. Hawaii
   B. California   D. Rhode Island

3. Which sentence is NOT true about the USA?
   A. Most of the states have four seasons.
   B. The size of each state is quite different.
   C. Most of the states are warm and dry.
   D. Some state names come from Native American languages.

Vocabulary
Use the words in the box to complete the sentences.

| continent | state | coast | temperature |
| population | climate | north | language |

1. Africa is not a country; it's a _____.
2. China has the highest _____ in the world.
3. What was the high _____ yesterday?
4. Texas has a very mild _____.
5. Washington, Oregon, and California are states on the West _____.
6. The USA is located to the _____ of Mexico.
7. Florida is a very warm _____.
8. There is no official _____ in the USA.

Activity

Origin of State Names

Many states in the USA have names that come from Native American languages. Other states were given their names by the Europeans who settled there. Surprisingly, only one state is named after an American person.

Look at the state names below. Match each one with its origin.

State Name	Origin
_____ 1. Mississippi	A. named for the Duke of York, who later became the King of England
_____ 2. Virginia	B. means "great water" in native language
_____ 3. Florida	C. named for the wife of King Charles of England
_____ 4. Michigan	D. means "red" in Spanish
_____ 5. Maryland	E. means "big river" in native language
_____ 6. Colorado	F. named for King Louis XIV of France
_____ 7. Georgia	G. named for the 1st president of the USA
_____ 8. Louisiana	H. named for Queen Elizabeth, the "Virgin Queen" of England
_____ 9. Washington	I. means "flowery" in Spanish
_____ 10. New York	J. named for King George II of England

Unit 2: The Original 13 Colonies

Warm Up

1. How is this flag different from the USA flag we see today?

2. Why are there 13 stars and 13 stripes on this flag?

3. Has the size of your country changed during its history?

Reading

The Original 13 Colonies

Today, the United States of America has 50 states. But, when the USA was a new country, it was not so big. At first, there were only 13 states; and before that, these areas belonged to England, or Britain. These states are often called the "original 13 colonies."

A colony is an area, including the people who live there, that is controlled by or belongs to another country that is usually far away from it. The original 13 colonies that became the USA were British colonies. At that time, Britain (or England) was one of the most powerful countries in the world. England had many colonies around the world, including parts of Canada, Africa, India, Ireland, and many small islands.

The 13 British colonies in North America were located along the East Coast—next to the Atlantic Ocean. The first British colony in the New World was Jamestown, Virginia. It was founded in 1607. Most of the settlers hoped to find gold in the New World, but life for these early settlers was very difficult. They did not find gold, and many of them died from hunger, disease, and battles with Native Americans.

The next important colony was the Massachusetts Bay colony. The settlers who came to Massachusetts—called Plymouth at that time—did not come for gold. They came because they wanted to live in a place where they could practice their religion freely. These early settlers were called "Pilgrims." Today, many Americans think of the Pilgrims as important founders of the modern USA.

By 1775, many of the people living in the 13 British colonies did not want to be part of Britain. They wanted to make their own country. In 1776, the leaders of the 13 colonies declared their independence and created the United States of America.

Quiz

Choose the best answer for each question.

1. Before 1776, what country controlled the 13 colonies in North America?
   A. Britain   C. the USA
   B. Canada   D. Virginia

2. Where was the first British colony in North America?
   A. Alaska   C. Massachusetts
   B. Canada   D. Virginia

3. Which sentence is NOT true about the original 13 colonies?
   A. The 13 colonies used to belong to Britain.
   B. The first settlers in North America found a lot of gold.
   C. Life was very hard for most of the first British settlers in the colonies.
   D. Britain's 13 colonies in North America eventually became the USA.

Vocabulary

Use the words in the box to complete the sentences.

country	founded	colony	settlers
British	created	England	religion

1. A _____ is land that is controlled by another country.

2. Jamestown, Virginia was _____ in 1607.

3. Most of the early _____ in Virginia wanted to find gold.

4. The "Pilgrims" came to America to practice their _____ freely.

5. India also used to be a _____ colony.

6. _____ is actually part of Britain, but the words are often used to mean the same thing.

7. The USA was _____ in 1776 when the colonies declared their independence.

8. Russia is the biggest _____ in the world.

Activity

The Original 13 Colonies

Look at the map below showing the original 13 colonies. Label and write the names of these colonies. The names are the same as the names of the states today.
Use the Internet or ask your teacher for help.

Original 13 Colonies			
1		8	
2		9	
3		10	
4		11	
5		12	
6		13	
7			

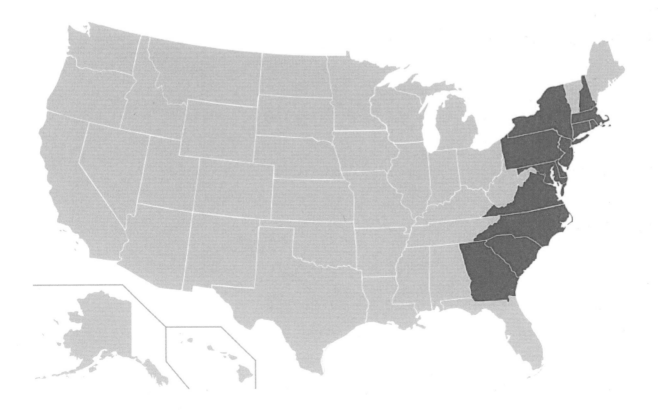

Unit 3: Bright Lights, Big Cities

Warm Up

1. Which do you like better: big cities or small towns? Why?

2. What's the biggest city you've ever been to?

3. How many cities in the USA can you name?

Reading

Bright Lights, Big Cities

The United States of America is a big country—the third largest country in the world. The USA also has the third largest population in the world—around 320 million people. Only China and India have more people.

When the USA was a young country, most of the people lived in rural areas, and farming was the most common occupation. Today, however, less than a quarter of the population lives in rural areas, and only about 2% of Americans are working in agriculture.

Starting in the 19th century, the population of American cities began to explode. As an example, Los Angeles had less than 100,000 people at the end of the 19th century. It was not a very big city. But, the city grew very quickly during the 20th century; and today, Los Angeles has a population of about 4 million people. It is the second biggest city in the USA.

The biggest city in the USA is, of course, New York City. The population of New York City is about 8.5 million. It has been the biggest city in the USA for a long time. It is also one of the most diverse cities in the world. People from nearly every country on earth live in New York City. You can walk down the street and hear people speaking many different languages. And you can eat in restaurants serving food from all parts of the world. Some people consider it to be the most important financial and cultural city in the world.

Today, the USA has 10 cities with more than a million people, and around 30 more with a population of at least half a million. The state with the most big cities is California. Los Angeles, San Diego, San Jose, San Francisco, Fresno, Sacramento, Long Beach, and Oakland all have populations of half a million people or more.

Despite its long history as an agrarian nation, more and more Americans are moving to urban areas.

Quiz

Choose the best answer for each question.

1. What is the current population of the United States?
   A. about 2%
   C. in the 20th century
   B. 8.5 million people
   D. around 320 million

2. What is the second biggest city in the USA?
   A. New York
   C. California
   B. Los Angeles
   D. Washington, D.C.

3. Which sentence is the best summary of the reading passage?
   A. The USA has the biggest cities in the world.
   B. Recently, more and more Americans are moving from cities to rural areas.
   C. New York City is the best place to live in America.
   D. The USA started as a small, agrarian nation, but now most people live in cities.

Vocabulary

Use the words in the box to complete the sentences.

population	rural	agriculture	century
financial	million	diverse	urban

1. I live in a really small town; it's a very _____ area.
2. _____ is the opposite of rural.
3. A _____ means one hundred years.
4. Some people say that New York is the _____ center of the world.
5. There are ten cities in the USA with more than a _____ people.
6. New York is a very _____ city.
7. I'm interested in farming; I want to study _____.
8. The _____ of New York City is about 8.5 million people.

Activity

Biggest Cities in the USA

1. Can you name some big cities in the USA? Work with a partner. Make a list of some big cities in the USA that you know.

_____	_____
_____	_____
_____	_____
_____	_____
_____	_____

2. Listen to your teacher. First, write the names of the ten biggest cities in the USA. Then, listen again and write the population.

	City	Population
1.		
2.		
3.		
4.		
5.		
6.		
7.		
8.		
9.		
10.		

Unit 4: Alaska and Hawaii

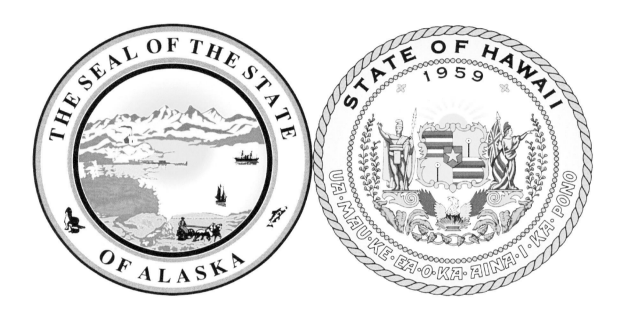

Warm Up

1. What's the most unique part of your country?

2. Name three differences between Alaska and Hawaii.

3. Which state would you rather visit: Alaska or Hawaii? Why?

Reading

Alaska and Hawaii

When most people imagine a map of the USA, they probably see something like the map in Unit 1 of this book. But, in addition to the Lower 48, there are several other pieces that make up the USA. Two of those biggest pieces are Alaska and Hawaii. Alaska and Hawaii were the 49th and 50th states to join the United States. They both became states in 1959.

Every state in the USA has something unique about it, but Alaska and Hawaii are probably the two most unique states. For starters, they are the only two states that don't share a border with another state. Alaska is located far north of the Lower 48. It would take about 48 hours to drive from Seattle, Washington to Anchorage, Alaska. Of course, you could fly or go by boat, too. Hawaii is located far out in the Pacific Ocean. It takes about 5 hours to fly from Los Angeles, California to Honolulu, Hawaii.

Besides being very far away from the rest of the USA, there are lots of other interesting and unique things about Alaska and Hawaii. Alaska is the biggest state in the USA. It's twice as big as the next biggest state—Texas. But, Alaska has a very small population. Only two other states have fewer people. Hawaii is small, but there are three states that are smaller than Hawaii. Hawaii also has more people than about 10 other states.

The most remarkable thing about both Alaska and Hawaii is probably the weather. Alaska is the coldest state in the USA. The average yearly temperature is around 32°F (or 0°C), and some parts of Alaska are frozen all year round. Hawaii, on the other hand, is the warmest state. Some people say that Hawaii has the most perfect weather in the world. It is never really cold—except at the top of a few mountains, where it occasionally snows—but it is also rarely very hot. It is a sunny and warm place all year round.

Quiz

Choose the best answer for each question.

1. What is the biggest state in the USA?
    A. Alaska   C. California
    B. Texas   D. Hawaii

2. Where is Hawaii located?
    A. in California   C. north of the Lower 48
    B. near Los Angeles   D. in the Pacific Ocean

3. Today, how many stars and stripes does the USA flag have?
    A. 13 stars and 13 stripes
    B. 13 stars and 50 stripes
    C. 50 stars and 13 stripes
    D. 50 stars and 50 stripes

Vocabulary

Use the words in the box to complete the sentences.

unique	border	located	remarkable
temperature	average	frozen	volcano

1. The USA and Canada share a long _____.
2. Canada is _____ to the north of the USA.
3. What's the _____ temperature in your hometown in summer?
4. What was the high _____ yesterday?
5. Ice is just _____ water.
6. The _____ erupted, sending ash and lava everywhere.
7. Have you read his story? I thought it was _____!
8. Venice, Italy is one of the most _____ cities in the world. There's no other city quite like it.

Activity

Alaska or Hawaii?

Read the list of sentences below. Decide if each sentence is about Alaska or Hawaii. Write the letter of the sentence in the correct box.

Alaska	Hawaii
___ ___ ___ ___	___ ___ ___ ___
___ ___ ___	___ ___ ___

A. Surfing is a very popular sport here.

B. Pineapples are grown here.

C. Native people are called Eskimos.

D. The USA bought it from Russia in 1867.

E. A royal family ruled here before it became part of the USA.

F. The first people here probably came from Siberia.

G. There are a lot of Japanese and Chinese living here.

H. It has the highest percent of native people of any state.

I. A lot of oil is produced here.

J. This state's nickname is the "Aloha State."

K. This state has a lot more men than women.

L. People here live longer than in any other state in the USA.

M. The highest mountain in the USA is here.

N. The biggest volcano in the world is here.

Unit 5: Columbus and the New World

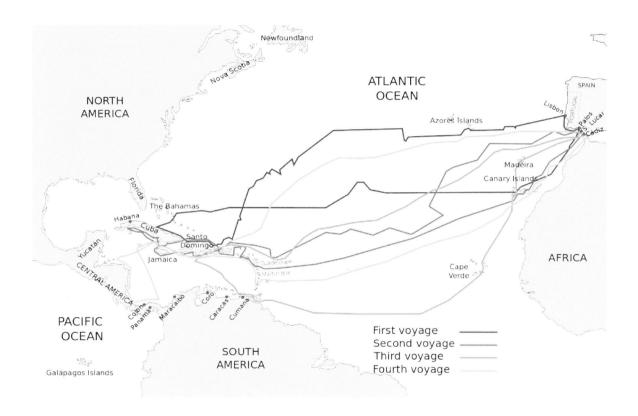

Warm Up

1. How many voyages did Columbus make to America?

2. Where did Columbus begin his voyages?

3. Where did Columbus actually want to go? and Why?

Reading

Columbus and the New World

Most humans in the 15th century did not know much about people who lived in other parts of the world. In fact, most people at this time rarely traveled far from their home during their lifetime. Thus, people living in Europe knew very little about Asia, and vice versa. People in Europe, Africa, and Asia didn't know about the continents of North and South America at all. Some people thought the world was flat and that ships would sail off the edge of the earth if they went too far.

Many people in Europe, however, wanted to trade for goods in Asia—things like spices, silk, and gold. But, travelling to Asia by land was dangerous and took a very long time. This was also the beginning of the Age of Discovery—a period in which European countries began using new ship designs and navigation techniques to explore the oceans. Previously, ocean travel was extremely difficult, dangerous, and full of myths about scary sea monsters.

In 1492, Christopher Columbus departed with three ships from Spain on a journey that would change the world. Columbus wanted to go to Asia; he believed that the earth was round and that he could get to Asia by sailing west across the Atlantic Ocean. After a difficult journey of ten weeks, Columbus reached land. But where was he? Columbus believed that he was in "the Indies"—islands close to India. That is why he called the native peoples living there "Indians." In fact, Columbus was not near India. He was in a "New World" unknown to Europeans.

Today, we know the island where Columbus first landed is part of the Bahamas. Columbus made three more voyages to the New World, exploring many islands in the Americas, but he never realized the truth about his discovery. He died still believing that he had reached Asia. His voyages, however, brought about important exchanges between the Old World and the New World. In the years that followed, Spain and other European countries took much gold and silver from the Americas, created huge colonies, and conquered the native peoples.

Quiz

Choose the best answer for each question.

1. What was the main reason for Columbus's voyage?
   A. He wanted to discover a New World.
   B. He wanted to prove to everyone that the world was round.
   C. He wanted to get valuable trade goods from Asia.
   D. He wanted to make a famous discovery.

2. How long did it take Columbus to reach the New World?
   A. four times   C. ten weeks
   B. about two weeks   D. 92 days

3. Where did Columbus arrive on his first voyage to the New World?
   A. the USA   C. some islands in the Americas
   B. the East Indies   D. Spain

Vocabulary

Use the words in the box to complete the sentences.

continent	voyage	discovery	spices
dangerous	unknown	conquer	ocean

1. Do you think of Europe and Asia as one _____ or two?
2. Columbus made his first _____ to America in 1492.
3. Europeans wanted to get silk and _____ from Asia.
4. Is there any place left on earth that is _____ to humans?
5. Some people think that Columbus's arrival in the New World should not be called a

   _____.

6. _____ means to take control of a place and/or group of people by fighting.
7. Travelling by ship in the 15th century was very _____.
8. Columbus sailed across the Atlantic _____.

19

Activity

Columbus: Hero or Villain?

Do you think Columbus is a "hero" or a "villain"?
First, write down some of the positive things about Columbus and his voyages to America.
Next, write down some of the negative things.
Which do you think are greater: the positive aspects or the negative aspects?
Write a paragraph explaining your point of view.

Christopher Columbus	
Hero / Positive aspects	**Villain / Negative aspects**

_____

_____

_____

_____

_____

_____

_____

_____

Unit 6: Native Americans

Warm Up

1. Why are Native Americans also called "Indians"?

2. Where did Native Americans originally come from?

3. Do you think we can see people like this in the USA today?

Reading

Nativ[e]

No one knows for sure how many [...] [Am]erica at the time of Columbus. Estimates range fr[o...] [real]ly know. We also don't know exactly how long peop[le...]

What we do know is that the first p[eople...fro]m Asia thousands of years ago. They came acro[ss...] [s]ea was much lower than it is now. These people [...] [s]ea and began moving down into North and South A[merica...]

By the time Columbus arrived in 149[2...] "[n]ative" Americans living in every part of the America[s...] ways of life. Some lived in small tribes as hunters and gatherers without any permanent houses. Other groups developed agriculture and lived together in communities. The largest civilization, the Aztecs in Mexico, had a capital city called Tenochtitlan that was one of the biggest cities in the world at that time.

The indigenous peoples of the Americas also spoke different languages; there were possibly as many as one thousand different languages. Some Native Americans were very peaceful; others were more aggressive and warlike.

However, all of these people had one thing in common. After the arrival of Europeans, their way of life began to decline. Guns, diseases, and land-hungry immigrants who came to America eventually destroyed the way of life of virtually every major indigenous group in the New World.

Today, Native Americans make up only about 1% of the population of the USA. Some Native Americans live on "reservations"—special land that the US government has reserved for them—but most of them choose to live and work in cities and towns, just like other American citizens.

(handwritten margin notes:)
estimates: guesses
reserved
crossed: moved from one side to another
gatherers:
permanent:
aggressive: warlike
decline: go down
destroyed:
virtually:

Quiz

Choose the best answer for each question.

1. How many Native Americans were living in the Americas in 1492?
   - A. about 200,000
   - B. 1 million
   - C. 10 million
   - D. No one knows for sure.

2. Where did the first Native Americans come from?
   - A. Asia
   - B. Canada
   - C. Europe
   - D. South America

3. What happened to most groups of indigenous people living in the Americas?
   - A. They moved to other areas after the Europeans came.
   - B. Most of them died in battles.
   - C. They mixed with Europeans and became US citizens.
   - D. Their land and way of life were taken away by Europeans.

Vocabulary

Use the words in the box to complete the sentences.

tribe	indigenous	peaceful	civilization
hunter	reservation	diseases	warlike

1. Many Native Americans died from _____.
2. Martin Luther King, Jr. was a _____ man; he did not believe in violence.
3. _____ means the opposite of peaceful.
4. The Aztecs had a very large and advanced _____.
5. A _____ kills animals for food.
6. Native and _____ both mean the same thing.
7. The Sioux were a powerful _____ of Indians who lived on the Great Plains.
8. Today, some Indians live on a _____, but many do not.

Activity

Words from Native American languages

There are lots of words and place names used in American English today that come from Native American languages. Look at the list of words and match each word with its meaning.

_____ 1. canoe	A. woma
_____ 2. barbecue	B. small
_____ 3. squaw	C. powe
_____ 4. chocolate	D. house
_____ 5. tomahawk	E. small
_____ 6. moccasin	F. oily, gr
_____ 7. persimmon	G. talk or
_____ 8. toboggan	H. starch
_____ 9. coyote	I. grill for
_____ 10. teepee	J. large g
_____ 11. wigwam	K. axe used for fighting
_____ 12. hammock	L. big deer with large antlers
_____ 13. hurricane	M. long snow sled
_____ 14. powwow	N. small boat
_____ 15. tomato	O. soft shoe
_____ 16. raccoon	P. orange fruit
_____ 17. potato	Q. drink or sweets made from cocoa
_____ 18. avocado	R. light, hanging net bed
_____ 19. iguana	S. red, fruity vegetable
_____ 20. moose	T. small animal related to a bear

Handwritten answers:

1. N   9. B   18 F
2. I   10. D   19. J
3. A   11. E   20 L
4. Q   12. R
5. K   13. C
6. O   14. G
7. P   15. S
8. M   16. T
        17. H

Unit 7: The USA is Born

Warm Up

1. What do you think is happening in this picture?

2. Who are the two groups that are fighting? Which is which?

3. When and where do you think this event took place?

Reading

The USA is Born

In the years after Columbus's discovery, European nations established colonies in North and South America. Spain made the first successful settlements in the New World. France and England also sent explorers to the New World.

As you read in Unit 2, by the 18th century, England had 13 colonies in North America along the Atlantic Ocean. Not all of the people living there were English. People also came from countries like Holland, Ireland, and Germany. Africans were also brought to America and forced to work as slaves. Waves of new settlers pushed the Indians west as the colonists' farms, towns, and cities grew.

Most of these colonists were content to be part of England. Slowly, however, a feeling of independence began to arise among them. Many colonists were unhappy about taxes they had to pay to the British government. "No taxation without representation," they cried. In 1773, a group of angry colonists in Massachusetts went onto a British ship and threw all of its tea into the sea as a protest against a tax on tea. This "Boston Tea Party" led to more trouble and bad feelings between the British government and the colonists in America.

In 1775, British soldiers met a group of American colonists in the village of Lexington, near Boston. Someone fired a shot—no one knows for sure which side fired first. It became the first battle in the American War of Independence. On July 4, 1776, American leaders officially declared their independence from England. They also used a new name—the United States of America. The "Declaration of Independence" not only stated that the 13 colonies were a new nation, it also explained their idea that people had a right to choose their own government.

The war between the new United States and England lasted for many years, and it looked at times as if the new nation would not succeed. But, under the leadership of George Washington, and with help from France, the Americans won the war. In 1783, England officially signed the treaty ending the war and recognizing its former colonies as a new nation. The USA was born.

Quiz

Choose the best answer for each question.

1. Why were many colonists in America unhappy with the British government?
   A. England was too far away.   C. The king never visited America.
   B. They had different religions.   D. They didn't want to pay British taxes.

2. When did Americans officially declare their independence from England?
   A. 1492   C. 1776
   B. 1775   D. 1783

3. How did the Americans win a war against such a powerful nation like Britain?
   A. The Americans had a lot more money than the British.
   B. George Washington was a good leader, and the French helped them.
   C. They destroyed the British army's tea, and then they had nothing to drink.
   D. England signed a treaty because they disliked fighting in wars.

Vocabulary

Use the words in the box to complete the sentences.

explorer	protest	soldiers	colonists
declare	independence	treaty	tax

1. Columbus was a great _____.
2. The British army had many well-trained _____.
3. _____ means to say something in a serious or formal way.
4. Both countries signed the _____ to end the war.
5. What is the sales _____ in your country?
6. The _____ living in North America were from many countries.
7. People sometimes take part in a _____ against something they dislike.
8. Americans gained their _____ by winning the war.

27

Activity

1492 and 1776

If you ask most Americans, they might say that they don't like history or know so much about it, but there are two dates that most Americans know. They are 1492 and 1776: Columbus's arrival in the New World and the Declaration of Independence. These are two of the most important historical events in America history.

What about in your country? What is the most important event in your country's history? Choose one event and write a short article about it. Try to answer all the basic question words in English: *Who? What? When? Where? Why?* and *How?*

_____

_____

_____

_____

_____

_____

_____

_____

_____

_____

_____

_____

Unit 8: Abraham Lincoln

Warm Up

1. What do you know about Abraham Lincoln?

2. Do you think he is similar to or different from Donald Trump?

3. Who is the greatest leader in the history of your country?

Reading

Abraham Lincoln

Abraham Lincoln was the 16th president of the United States, from 1861 to 1865. Many Americans think that he was the greatest president in U.S. history. He is one of four presidents—along with George Washington, Thomas Jefferson, and Teddy Roosevelt—whose face is carved on Mount Rushmore.

Lincoln was born into a poor family. As a child, he lived in a very simple log cabin. He studied and worked hard. He became a lawyer, and then he entered politics. The story of his life is often used to show that, in the USA, anyone who works hard can grow up to achieve greatness.

Lincoln was a great president, but he served as president during one of the most difficult times in American history. This was the time of the Civil War. For a long time, Americans had been arguing about the issue of slavery. Many Americans—mostly those living in the North—wanted to abolish slavery. Most people living in the South, however, wanted to keep slavery.

Lincoln was from the North. He wanted the United States to stay together as one country. Shortly after he was elected president in 1860, the Southern states decided to secede, or leave, the USA. They wanted to make their own nation. Lincoln refused to let them go.

In 1861, the American Civil War began. The war divided friends and families. Brothers fought and killed each other. Lincoln's own brother-in-law died fighting for the South. It was the deadliest war in US history. More Americans died in this war than in all other wars in U.S. history combined.

The Civil War lasted four long years. When the war ended, the North won and slavery was abolished. However, just a few days after the war ended, Lincoln was shot and killed while he was watching a play in a theater.

The tragic Civil War was over, and the issue of slavery was also now ended in America, but the country had lost one of its greatest leaders.

Quiz

Choose the best answer for each question.

1. How long did the Civil War last?
    A. about one year   C. six years
    B. four years   D. longer than all other wars combined

2. What happened after the North won the Civil War?
    A. Slavery was abolished in the United States.
    B. The Southern states made their own nation.
    C. Lincoln became the 16th president of the United States.
    D. Lincoln refused to let the Southern states back in the USA.

3. Which US president's face is NOT on Mount Rushmore?
    A. Abraham Lincoln   C. Franklin Roosevelt
    B. George Washington   D. Teddy Roosevelt

Vocabulary

Use the words in the box to complete the sentences.

slavery	abolish	struggle	brother-in-law
secede	elected	divided	issue

1. Your sister's husband is your _____.

2. It was a real _____ for me to lose weight.

3. The class was _____ on the question; some agreed, but others did not.

4. Now, the _____ of gay marriage is being debated in some countries.

5. Donald Trump was _____ president in 2016.

6. Lincoln wanted to _____, or end, slavery.

7. The Southern states decided to _____, or leave, the USA after Lincoln was elected.

8. _____ was abolished, or ended, in the USA in 1865.

Ac   1. B
      2. A   burg Address
      3. C

The   that Abraham Lincoln gave after a terrible
batt   t is considered one of the greatest speeches in
US

The   n 1863, so we don't really know what Lincoln
sou   of people performing this speech on the
Inte

Read the words of the speech. (This isn't the whole speech.) Practice saying it out loud.
Have a speech or recitation contest in your class.

"Four score and seven years ago our fathers brought forth on this continent a new nation, conceived in liberty, and dedicated to the proposition that all men are created equal.

Now we are engaged in a great civil war, testing whether that nation, or any nation so conceived, can long endure. We are met on a great battlefield of that war. We have come to dedicate that field, as a final resting place for those who gave their lives that that nation might live.

The world will little note, nor long remember what we say here, but it can never forget what they did here. It is for us the living, to be dedicated to the unfinished work which they who fought here have thus far so nobly advanced. It is for us to be dedicated to the great task remaining before us—that these dead shall not have died in vain—that this nation, under God, shall have a new birth of freedom—and that government of the people, by the people, for the people, shall not perish from the earth."

Unit 9: The Wild West

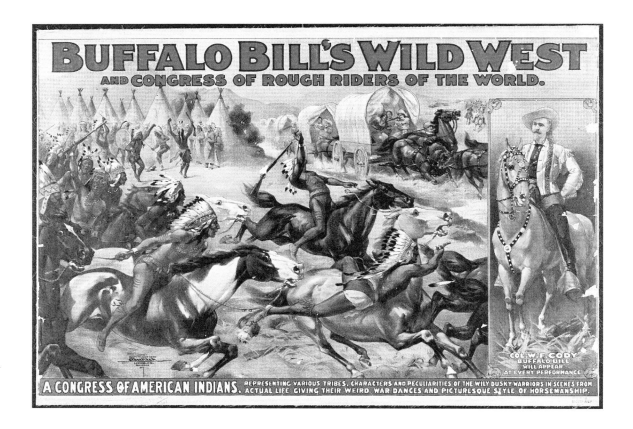

Warm Up

1. What do you think "The Wild West" means?

2. Describe what you see on this poster.

3. Do you think scenes like this one are more fact or fiction?

Reading

The Wild West

As we read in Unit 2 and 7, the first states in the USA were all located on the East Coast. The area west of the towns and villages where American settlers lived was known as the "frontier." The frontier was often a wild and dangerous place. As more and more people—mostly Europeans—came to North America, they kept pushing the frontier farther and farther west. The early history of the USA is largely the story of the United States expanding across the "Wild West."

After Americans won the War of Independence, Britain agreed to give them all of the land up to the Mississippi River. The next major piece of the USA is known as the "Louisiana Purchase." It was a huge piece of land that France sold to the USA in 1803. It nearly doubled the size of the USA.

As the USA grew, and Americans spread across their new lands, a feeling that all of North America was destined to be part of the USA became popular. Texas was the next part to join the USA. After a war with Mexico in 1848, the USA took another huge piece of land known as the "Mexican Cession." Oregon also became part of the USA when a treaty with Britain decided the border between what is now Canada and the USA.

Life in these new parts of the USA was very different than life in the towns and cities on the East Coast. Wild animals, Native Americans, and extreme weather conditions made life on the frontier very hard.

The "Wild West" was a time when explorers, hunters, and trappers moved across the western part of the USA. It was the era of cowboys and gunfighters. It is remembered as a time when Indians fought with white settlers. Gold was discovered in California, and thousands of people from all over the world rushed there to get rich. And many pioneer families left the old world behind and moved across the continent searching for a new way of life.

The Wild West era ended around 1890 when there was no more frontier left in the USA. It was a remarkable time in American history. It was a time that helped to shape the American character. The hard work, freedom, opportunity, and self-reliance of this era became a major part of American culture.

Quiz

Choose the best answer for each question.

1. What country did the USA buy Louisiana from?
   A. Britain
   B. France
   C. Spain
   D. Russia

2. Where was gold discovered?
   A. Boston
   B. California
   C. Mexico
   D. Louisiana

3. Which sentence is NOT true about the Wild West?
   A. As America grew, the frontier constantly moved westward.
   B. Thousands of people rushed to California after gold was discovered.
   C. The Wild West era helped to shape American culture.
   D. Indians stopped Americans from expanding across the continent.

Vocabulary

Use the words in the box to complete the sentences.

frontier	huge	destined	self-reliance
trapper	cowboys	pioneer	settlers

1. A _____ is a person who catches animals and sells their fur.

2. _____ are people who go to live in a new, undeveloped place.

3. A _____ is like a settler; it's a person who is one of the first to move to a new place or try a new thing.

4. Russia is a _____ country.

5. Many Americans believed the USA was _____ to control all of North America.

6. By about 1890, there was no more _____ in the USA.

7. _____ are one of the symbols of the American Wild West.

8. _____ means being able to do everything by yourself.

Activity

Look at the map ~~s~~ ... ~~ates~~ ... ~~rt~~ below showing how and when
each part entered ... your teacher for help.

Handwritten notes (overlaid):

```
1. B
2. B
3. D

1) trapper          5) destined
2) settlers            frontier
3) pioneer          6) cowboys
4) huge             7) cowboys
                    8) self-reliance

2. Louisiana
3. bought from Sp 1821
4. Texas → added 1845
5. treaty decided border
   w/ Canada — 1846
6. Mexican Cession
7. purchase from Mexico 1853
8. purchased from Russia 1867
9. Hawaii
```

		how and when
1	U.S.A. (new nation)	treaty with Britain in 1783
2		bought from France in 1803
3	Florida	
4		
5	Oregon	
6		won in a war with Mexico in 1848
7	Gadsden Purchase	
8	Alaska	
9		annexed in 1898

Unit 10: The American Century

Warm Up

1. Do you know where and when this photo was taken?

2. Why is the 20th century sometimes called the "American Century"?

3. Do you think the USA is still the most powerful country in the world?

Reading

The American Century

As we read in Unit 9, the United States grew from a small country in 1783 to a huge country by the end of the 19th century. And in the 20th century, the USA grew to be the world's strongest economic and military country. For this reason, the 20th century is sometimes called the "American Century."

For much of human history, India and China had the biggest populations and the world's largest economies. In the late 19th century, Britain had the world's largest empire and the most powerful navy in the world. The young USA was just a small, growing country, but not one that other nations thought of as a world leader.

By 1900, however, the USA had grown to the fourth largest population in the world, and its economy had also become the largest in the world. The answer to how the USA became such a successful and powerful nation is long and complicated. What we can say simply is that the USA is a very unique and fortunate country.

First, the USA is a colorful and lively mix of people and cultures. Out of these people came ambition, creativity, and effort. The USA is also blessed with great natural resources and two oceans to protect it. Finally, the USA developed a system of government that gave its people peace and freedom. With all these things, Americans in the 20th century achieved amazing growth and innovation.

Wars in Europe destroyed land, lives, and industries. The USA, on the other hand, was never invaded. After World War 2, the USA—along with Russia—was now clearly a world "superpower." When the "Cold War" ended, the USA was left alone as the most powerful nation on earth.

But the American Century is more than just about winning wars and a powerful economy. It was the spread of American culture that added to the influence of the United States. American TV programs and movies were shown all over the world. American food and supermarkets became popular worldwide. People in other countries loved blue jeans, Mickey Mouse, rock-and-roll, and Apple computers. This "soft power" of the USA may, indeed, be the most powerful aspect of the American Century.

Quiz

Choose the best answer for each question.

1. Which country had the world's largest empire in the 19th century?
   A. Russia
   C. China
   B. Britain
   D. the USA

2. Which two countries were called "superpowers" after World War 2?
   A. Russia and China
   C. China and India
   B. Britain and France
   D. Russia and the USA

3. Which sentence is NOT true about the "American Century"?
   A. American TV and movies spread US culture around the world.
   B. Wars destroyed many things in other countries, but not in the USA.
   C. Life was very hard and dangerous for most Americans in the 20th century.
   D. By 1900, the USA already had the world's largest economy.

Vocabulary

Use the words in the box to complete the sentences.

century	decade	economy	military
empire	culture	resources	influence

1. A _____ is 10 years.
2. A _____ is 100 years.
3. The USA has a lot of natural _____.
4. Each country has its own unique _____.
5. England had the world's largest _____ in the 19th century.
6. Music and TV have a big _____ on many young people.
7. The USA has, by far, the world's largest _____.
8. Japan's _____ grew incredibly fast during the Cold War era.

Activity

Decades of the 20ᵗʰ Century

Match each decade with the events that happened in it.

_____ 1900s	**A.** John F. Kennedy was elected president. He was shot and killed three years later. His brother Robert and Martin Luther King, Jr. were also killed during this turbulent decade. The USA landed the first men on the moon.
_____ 1910s	**B.** Bill Clinton was president for most of this decade. The US fought in the First Gulf War against Iraq. The US stock market soared, and the USA appeared to be stronger than ever.
_____ 1920s	**C.** The USA was still in the middle of the Great Depression. Franklin Roosevelt won the first of his four presidential elections. The Empire State Building in New York became the world's tallest building.
_____ 1930s	**D.** The Wright brothers flew the world's first airplane. Henry Ford produced his first Ford Model T car. The USA became the world's biggest economy. The "American Century" was just beginning.
_____ 1940s	**E.** The USA entered World War 2. Scientists in the USA built the world's first atomic bomb. The USA and Russia defeated Hitler in Germany; the USA dropped 2 atomic bombs on Japan. The United Nations was formed.
_____ 1950s	**F.** The Titanic sank on its first voyage from England to the USA. Henry Ford used the assembly line to build cheap, reliable cars. The USA helped England and France win World War 1.
_____ 1960s	**G.** Richard Nixon became the first US president ever to resign. Bill Gates started Microsoft, and a year later Steve Jobs started Apple. The USA celebrated its bicentennial.
_____ 1970s	**H.** Women in the USA got the right to vote. Mickey Mouse appeared in his first movie. The stock market crashed at the end of this decade, which led to the Great Depression.
_____ 1980s	**I.** Ronald Reagan was a popular president. The Cold War ended when the Berlin Wall came down. The USA started the Space Shuttle program. The first Apple Macintosh computer was released.
_____ 1990s	**J.** The first Disneyland opened in California; the first McDonald's opened, also in California. The Supreme Court decided that all American schools must be integrated (i.e. Blacks and whites must attend the same schools.)

Unit 11: We the People

Warm Up

1. What do you think a "typical American" looks like?

2. What does the word "diversity" mean?

3. What races or ethnic groups do you see in this picture?

Reading

We the People

The United States is one of the most diverse countries in the world. In the USA, you will find people who come from nearly every place on earth.

As we read in Unit 2, the first, or native, Americans came from Asia a long time ago. But, today, Native Americans make up only about 1% of the population.

The largest group of people in the USA are "white" Americans. Most of these people are descendants of European immigrants. Most of the settlers who came to North America during the colonial period were British. As a result, English became the common language spoken in the USA.

Millions of Africans were also brought to North America as slaves during the colonial era. Though some "blacks" lived as free Americans, most of them were treated as property and forced to work as slaves. As we read in Unit 8, slavery was abolished after the Civil War. A few years later, in 1868, all African Americans became citizens of the United States.

In the 19th century, a new wave of immigrants began to arrive from countries like Ireland and Germany. Near the end of the 19th century, more and more immigrants came from countries in southern and eastern Europe—countries like Italy and Poland.

Immigrants came from many different places and for many different reasons. Some immigrants were escaping political or religious trouble in their home countries. But, the most important reason has generally been economic. People have immigrated to the USA in hopes of finding a higher standard of living and greater opportunities.

However, immigrating to the USA was not always easy. Immigrants often faced prejudice and discrimination. They lived in crowded slums and worked long hours for low wages. Still, they wanted to stay in America because they were free. They could vote, and their children could go to school.

Today, there are more immigrants than ever before. The largest numbers of today's immigrants do not come from Europe. They come from Latin America and Asia—from countries such as Mexico and Cuba, China and Vietnam.

Immigration is sometimes a controversial issue in the USA. What we can say for sure, though, is that the United States is, and has always been, a nation of immigrants.

Quiz

Choose the best answer for each question.

1. During the colonial period, where did most North American immigrants come from?
   A. Africa   C. China
   B. Britain   D. Mexico

2. Which is the largest group of people in the USA?
   A. white Americans C. Hispanics
   B. black Americans D. Native Americans

3. What is the main reason that immigrants came to the United States?
   A. They wanted to find gold and other treasures.
   B. They came to the USA because they wanted to learn English.
   C. They were escaping from wars and disasters in their countries.
   D. They were hoping to find better economic opportunities.

Vocabulary

Use the words in the box to complete the sentences.

diverse	descendants	citizens	political
prejudice	controversial	vote	immigrants

1. _____ are people who move to another country.
2. Most Americans are _____ of immigrants.
3. Some immigrants experienced a lot of _____ in America.
4. In the USA, all _____ have the same rights.
5. American citizens can _____ in elections when they are 18 years old.
6. Americans are free to participate in the _____ process.
7. Gun control is a very _____ topic in the USA.
8. Today, the USA is a very _____ country.

Activity

Race and Ethnicity in the USA

The USA is a very racially and ethnically diverse nation. According to the US census (which is taken every ten years), Americans can choose from six main races and ethnicities when answering the census questions. A "race" is usually thought to include things like skin color and other physical characteristics, while "ethnicity" refers more to a person's cultural background.

What do you think those six races and ethnic groups are? (Hint: Go back and check the Reading) Write your answers in the box; then [...] percentage of the US population you think each g[...]

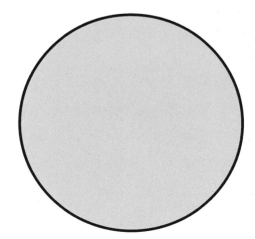

	Races and ethnic groups in the USA
1	
2	
3	
4	
5	
6	

1. whites   61%
2. Latinos   18%
3. Afr. Amers.   13%
4. Asians   6%
5. Native Amea   1%
6. Native Hawaiians   .2%

Now, listen to your teacher. Write the correct answers in the box, and make a new pie chart based on the percentages your teacher tells you.

	Races and ethnic groups in the USA
1	
2	
3	
4	
5	
6	

Unit 12: Washington, D.C.

Warm Up

1. What is the capital city of the United States?

2. What is the capital of your country? Have you been there?

3. What is the building in the picture? What happens there?

Reading

Washington, D.C.

The capital city of the United States is Washington, D.C. Washington, D.C. isn't part of any state. It is located between Maryland and Virginia. "D.C." stands for the "District of Columbia." It's a "federal district" completely under control of the US government. It was named after the first president of the USA, George Washington.

Washington, D.C. is the location of all "three branches" of the US government: the executive, the legislative, and the judicial. One of the main ideas of the US government is the system of "checks and balances" between these three branches. Each branch has certain powers, but these powers are balanced and checked by the others so that none of the three branches can become too powerful.

The "executive branch" is made up of the president and his cabinet. The president of the USA lives in the White House in Washington, D.C. The president leads the country and is also the "commander-in-chief" of the armed forces. The president is elected by the people and can be elected to a maximum of two 4-year terms.

The "legislative branch" is made up of the Congress. The US Congress has two parts: the House of Representatives and the Senate. The House of Representatives is made of representatives from all the states. States with more people have more representatives. For example, California—the most populous state—currently has 53 representatives. There are seven states with only 1 representative each because they have so few people. In the Senate, however, each state has 2 senators. The smallest states have just as much voice as the largest states. The main duty of the Congress is to make the laws of the country.

The "judicial branch" is made up of the Supreme Court and other federal courts. The courts settle disputes and decide whether laws must be followed or not.

No system of government is perfect, of course. Americans often argue about how to best organize and run their government, but many Americans also believe that their government is among the best ever in human history.

Quiz

Choose the best answer for each question.

1. What state is the capital city of the USA in?
   A. Maryland
   B. Virginia
   C. Washington
   D. It's not in any state.

2. What's the longest time that someone can be president of the USA?
   A. 4 years
   B. 6 years
   C. 8 years
   D. 16 years

3. Which statement is NOT true about the US government?
   A. The President of the USA has more power than the other branches.
   B. The US Congress has two parts: the House and the Senate.
   C. All three branches of the US government are located in Washington, D.C.
   D. Some states have more representatives than others in the government.

Vocabulary

Use the words in the box to complete the sentences.

capital	federal	elected	representative
court	executive	legislative	judicial

1. Ottawa is the _____ of Canada.
2. _____ has the same meaning as central or national.
3. The US President is _____ every four years.
4. The president is the head of the _____ branch.
5. The _____ branch is made of the federal courts.
6. The _____ branch makes the laws of the country.
7. Alaska has a very small population, so it has only one _____.
8. If you are arrested, you will probably have to go to _____.

Activity

Are you Patriotic?

Talk to your classmates. Go around the room and ask lots of questions. Try to find one person to complete each sentence. (Write the person's name in the blank.)
  e.g. *"Excuse me. Do you think the USA is the best country in the world?"*

Find someone who …

1. _____ thinks the USA is the best country in the world.

2. _____ thinks that his/her country is the best in the world.

3. _____ would like to live in another country someday.

4. _____ thinks that maybe Norway or Sweden is a better place to live than either his/her country or the USA.

5. _____ isn't very patriotic.

6. _____ likes to sing his/her country's national anthem.

7. _____ knows the name of the US national anthem.

8. _____ likes his/her country's flag.

9. _____ can explain the design of the US flag.

10. _____ feels patriotic when he/she watches the Olympics.

11. _____ loves his/her hometown.

12. _____ doesn't really like his/her hometown so much.

13. _____ admires the USA.

14. _____ thinks Americans are too patriotic.

15. _____ would like to change his/her nationality.

Unit 13: Martin Luther King, Jr.

Warm Up

1. What do you know about Martin Luther King, Jr?

2. Do you know the name of his most famous speech?

3. Why do you suppose he is a "hero" in America?

Reading

Martin Luther King, Jr.

Martin Luther King, Jr. is one of only three people to have a holiday named after him in the USA. The others are Christopher Columbus and George Washington. We all know that Columbus "discovered" America and that Washington was the first president. But, what did Martin Luther King, Jr. do?

King was born in Atlanta, Georgia in 1929. Even though black Americans were supposed to be free and equal citizens of the United States, this was not really true. Especially in the South, where King was born and raised, blacks faced a lot of discrimination—unfair treatment—from white Americans.

In many states, it was against the law for a black person to marry a white person. Black and white children went to different schools. Black people had to sit in different parts of restaurants and movie theaters. In many cities, blacks had to sit in the back of the bus. This system of separating the races was known as "segregation."

King began to fight against segregation as a young Baptist minister in 1955. When a black woman named Rosa Parks was arrested for refusing to give up her seat on a bus to a white passenger, King and other black leaders organized a boycott of the city buses. The Montgomery Bus Boycott lasted for over one year. King was arrested, and his house was bombed. But, he never stopped fighting for what he believed was right.

After the bus boycott, King became a well-known civil rights leader. "Civil rights" refers to the basic human rights of freedom and social, legal, and economic equality. King believed that all humans are equal. He wanted black people to have the same rights and freedoms as other Americans. To achieve this, he organized non-violent protests against segregation.

In 1963, during an event known as the March on Washington, King delivered his most famous speech—the "I Have a Dream" speech. Because of his powerful, yet peaceful, efforts to end segregation, King was awarded the Nobel Peace Prize in 1964. The same year, the USA passed the Civil Rights Act, which outlawed discrimination based on race, sex, religion, or national origin.

And because of these efforts, Americans today celebrate Martin Luther King, Jr. Day as a holiday to remember that all Americans are equal.

Quiz
Choose the best answer for each question.

1. What part of the USA was Martin Luther King, Jr. from?
   A. the East Coast   C. the West
   B. the South   D. Washington, D.C.

2. What was name of Martin Luther's King, Jr.'s most famous speech?
   A. I Have a Dream   C. March on Washington
   B. Civil Rights Act   D. Montgomery Bus Boycott

3. Which statement is NOT true about Martin Luther King, Jr.?
   A. King won the Nobel Peace Prize.
   B. Today, there is a holiday in the USA named after King.
   C. King faced a lot of discrimination when he was growing up.
   D. King was arrested because he refused to give his seat on the bus to a white person.

Vocabulary
Use the words in the box to complete the sentences.

equal	segregation	arrested	boycott
rights	discrimination	outlawed	protests

1. Separating people because of their race is known as _____.
2. Slavery was _____ after the Civil War.
3. Even though blacks were US citizens, they faced a lot of _____.
4. King and other leaders organized a _____ of the city buses.
5. Rosa Parks was _____ when she refused to give up her seat on the bus.
6. King organized effective _____ against segregation.
7. The US Constitution says that "all men are created _____."
8. King is best known as a civil _____ leader.

Activity

I Have a Dream

In 1963, one hundred years after Lincoln's "Gettysburg Address," Martin Luther King, Jr. made his famous "I Have a Dream" speech. (This is just a small part of his speech.)

"I say to you today, my friends, so even though we face the difficulties of today and tomorrow, I still have a dream. It is a dream deeply rooted in the American dream. I have a dream that one day this nation will rise up and live out the true meaning of its creed: 'We hold these truths to be self-evident: that all men are created equal.'

I have a dream that one day on the red hills of Georgia the sons of former slaves and the sons of former slave owners will be able to sit down together at the table of brotherhood.

I have a dream that one day even the state of Mississippi, a state sweltering with the heat of injustice, sweltering with the heat of oppression, will be transformed into an oasis of freedom and justice.

I have a dream that my four little children will one day live in a nation where they will not be judged by the color of their skin but by the content of their character. I have a dream today.

I have a dream that one day, down in Alabama, little black boys and black girls will be able to join hands with little white boys and white girls as sisters and brothers. I have a dream today."

Write a short answer to this question:
Do you think that King's dream has come true? Why or why not?

_____

_____

_____

_____

Unit 14: Motor City

Warm Up

1. What city in the USA is known as "Motor City"?

2. Do you have a driver's license? How often do you drive?

3. Which do you prefer: driving or using public transportation?

Reading

Motor City

There is some debate about who invented the first automobile. It's hard to say who made the first car partly because it's hard to define what a "car" is. In the USA, Henry Ford is considered to be the father of the modern automobile.

Ford did not invent the automobile, but he was the first person to manufacture cars that ordinary people could buy. Before that time, automobiles were strange machines that wealthy, eccentric people played with. Ford changed the automobile from a rich man's toy into a practical machine that transformed the American way of life.

Henry Ford was born on a farm in Michigan in 1863. Like many great Americans, he was the child of immigrant parents. His father came to the USA from Ireland, and his mother's family had come from Belgium. Ford did not like farm work. As a young man, he left the family farm and got a job in Detroit.

Around 1893, Ford began building engines and self-propelled vehicles. In 1896, he invented an "automobile" that he called the "Ford Quadricycle." That same year, Ford met the great American inventor Thomas Edison. Edison told Ford to continue making cars.

Although Ford experimented with many types of vehicles, including racing cars, his dream was to manufacture inexpensive automobiles that average Americans could afford. In 1908, his dream came true when the Ford Motor Company introduced the Model T. The car was easy to drive and take care of. Best of all, it was cheap—much cheaper than other cars at that time.

Sales of Ford's cars skyrocketed, and the Model T became the most popular car in America. More and more cars were needed to meet the demand. Ford became one of the largest and most successful companies in the world, and Detroit became the center of automobile manufacturing in the USA.

Today, the Ford Motor Company still has its headquarters in Detroit, Michigan. It is now the second-largest car company in the USA, after General Motors, which is also headquartered in Detroit.

And Americans love driving just as much as ever. Gasoline is cheap, most highways are free, and Americans enjoy the freedom that having a car gives them. Unfortunately, all those cars and drivers also create congestion. Some people say the USA has the worst traffic in the world.

Quiz

Choose the best answer for each question.

1. What was the name of Henry Ford's first automobile?
   A. Model T   C. Quadricycle
   B. Cadillac   D. Skyrocket

2. Why was the Ford Model T so popular?
   A. It was black.   C. It was fast.
   B. It was simple.   D. It was cheap.

3. Which sentence best describes Henry Ford's dream?
   A. He wanted to build the fastest car in the world.
   B. He wanted to be a great inventor like Thomas Edison.
   C. He wanted to build cars that ordinary Americans could afford.
   D. He wanted to make Detroit the center of the automobile industry.

Vocabulary

Use the words in the box to complete the sentences.

automobile	invented	ordinary	manufacture
vehicle	skyrocket	headquarters	congestion

1. An _____ is the same thing as a car. They mean the same thing.

2. Is there a lot of _____ on the roads where you live?

3. Thomas Edison _____ many amazing things.

4. Ford Motor Company's _____ are in Detroit, Michigan.

5. Henry Ford wanted to _____ inexpensive automobiles.

6. Ford's first _____ looked more like a bicycle than a car.

7. The Model T was so cheap that many _____ people could buy it.

8. If you make a great product and sell it at a cheap price, your sales will probably _____.

55

Activity

American English vs. British English

Sometimes American English and British English are different. Spelling, pronunciation, and vocabulary can be different in the two countries.

Cars are a good example. There are many different words in American English and British English when talking about cars and car parts.

Look at the words below. First, match the American and British words that mean the same thing. You can also write the word used in your native language. Is it similar to the American word or the British word?

Automobile vocabulary

American English	British English	my language
1. steering wheel	A. boot	
2. stick shift	B. motorway	
3. gas pedal	C. lorry	
4. hood	D. petrol	
5. trunk	E. accelerator	
6. windshield	F. silencer	
7. headlights	G. car park	
8. muffler	H. driving wheel	
9. sedan	I. windscreen	
10. truck	J. manual	
11. parking lot	K. saloon	
12. highway	L. bonnet	
13. gas	M. headlamps	

Unit 15: Hollywood

Warm Up

1. Have you seen a good movie recently?

2. Do you prefer watching movies in English or in your language?

3. What movie do you want to see next?

Reading

Hollywood

Most people around the world like watching movies. They entertain us, make us laugh, or sometimes cry. Movies inspire us and move us. Sometimes they frighten us, or keep us on the edge of our seat in suspense.

Americans love movies, too. More money is spent on movies—both making them and by movie goers—in the USA than in any other country. China and Japan are second and third in terms of money spent, but India actually has the largest number of movie goers in the world.

Hollywood is the center of the movie industry in the USA. The major film studios in Hollywood have produced many of the most successful movies of all time and had a powerful effect on the cinema industry around the world. Today, nearly everyone recognizes the name "Hollywood" as the place where movies are made.

But, in 1900, Hollywood was just a tiny town. There was only one hotel, a post office, and some farms. In 1910, Hollywood became part of Los Angeles. A few years later, a small movie studio opened. It was an ideal place to make movies because of the low costs and warm weather all year round. Soon, other movie studios moved to California. The rest, as they say, is history.

Every year, there is an awards ceremony in Hollywood known as the Academy Awards, or Oscars. Awards are given for the best movie of the year, best actor and actress, and best director, among other things. This ceremony is now anticipated and watched by people all over the world.

Katherine Hepburn is the only person to win four Best Actress awards. Daniel Day-Lewis is the only man to win Best Actor three times. Meryl Streep was nominated a record 15 times, and she has won twice.

Steven Spielberg is one of the most well-known movie directors in Hollywood. Spielberg won the Academy Award for Best Director two times—for *Schindler's List* in 1993 and *Saving Private Ryan* in 1998. Many of his films became "blockbusters" and broke records for number of sales. Some of his most famous and record-setting films are *Jaws*, *E.T. the Extra-Terrestrial*, *Jurassic Park*, and the *Indiana Jones* series.

Quiz

Choose the best answer for each question.

1. Which country has the most movie goers in the world?
   A. USA
   B. China
   C. Japan
   D. India

2. Who has won the most Academy Awards?
   A. Leonardo DiCaprio
   B. Daniel Day-Lewis
   C. Katherine Hepburn
   D. Steven Spielberg

3. Which sentence is NOT true about Hollywood?
   A. In 1900, Hollywood was not a well-known place.
   B. Hollywood is part of New York City.
   C. Hollywood was a good place to make movies because of the weather.
   D. Today, most people recognize Hollywood as the home of movie-making.

Vocabulary

Use the words in the box to complete the sentences.

industry	studio	cinema	ceremony
actor	actress	director	blockbuster

1. Something that is great and successful is called a _____.
2. The Academy Awards _____ is held every year in Hollywood.
3. Leonardo DiCaprio is my favorite _____.
4. Who is the most famous movie _____ in your country?
5. Do you know Meryl Streep? I think she's a great _____.
6. The first movie _____ in Hollywood opened in 1912.
7. A _____ is another word for a movie theater, or it could refer to the movie industry itself.
8. Hollywood is the center of the movie _____ in the USA.

Activity

Movie Quotes

Lines, or quotes, from movies sometimes become so popular that many people know and use them even if they haven't seen the movie.

Listed below are some well-known movie quotes in the USA. Have you heard these lines? Match them with the movie that they first appeared in.

Movie Quotes	Movie Title
1. "May the force be with you." _____	A. Jaws
2. "To infinity and beyond." _____	B. The Wizard of Oz
3. "I'll be back." _____	C. Sudden Impact
4. "Houston, we have a problem." _____	D. Casablanca
5. "You're gonna need a bigger boat." _____	E. Snow White
6. "You can't handle the truth." _____	F. Pinocchio
7. "We're not in Kansas anymore." _____	G. A Few Good Men
8. "You talkin' to me?" _____	H. The Terminator
9. "I'll make him an offer he can't refuse." _____	I. Gone With the Wind
10. "Always let your conscience be your guide." _____	J. The Godfather
11. "Heigh-ho, heigh-ho. It's off to work we go." _____	K. E.T.
12. "Go ahead, make my day." _____	L. Apollo 13
13. "Here's looking at your, kid." _____	M. Taxi Driver
14. "Frankly, my dear, I don't give a damn." _____	N. Star Wars
15. "E.T. phone home." _____	O. Toy Story

Unit 16: Burgers and Fries

Warm Up

1. What food do you eat the most often?

2. How often do you eat hamburgers and french fries?

3. What's your favorite fast food restaurant? How often do you go there?

Reading

Burgers and Fries

What food comes to mind when you think of American food? Many people probably think of hamburgers. Other American foods include things like hot dogs, popcorn, fried chicken, apple pie, peanut butter, corn flakes, and chocolate chip cookies.

Some of these foods weren't really created in America, but they became popular in the USA or were changed in America into the kind of food we recognize today. Hamburgers, along with their usual serving of french fries, are probably the most stereotypical of these American foods.

The word "hamburger" comes from Hamburg, a city in Germany. A "Hamburg steak" is a ground beef patty. It was probably in the USA that this meat was first put inside a bread roll, or bun. The first hamburgers are said to have been served at the 1904 World's Fair in St. Louis, Missouri. But, no one really knows exactly who made or ate the first "hamburger."

What we do know is that hamburgers became popular across the USA in the 20th century. White Castle was the first restaurant chain to sell hamburgers. The first shop opened in 1921. White Castle sold small, square burgers called "sliders." You can still find White Castle restaurants across the USA.

The most famous hamburger restaurant in the USA is McDonald's. The first shop was opened by the McDonald brothers—Maurice and Richard—in 1940 in San Bernardino, California. The McDonald brothers perfected the "fast food" system that other restaurants like White Castle had started.

Today, there are McDonald's restaurants in over a hundred countries all over the world serving millions of hamburgers every day. There are many other popular fast food hamburger chains in the USA, such as Burger King, Wendy's, In-N-Out Burger, Jack in the Box, and Shake Shack, just to name a few.

Americans also enjoy making and eating hamburgers at home. Burgers on the grill is an American favorite at picnics and barbecues. Popular things to put on hamburgers include cheese, lettuce, tomato, pickles, onions, ketchup, mustard, and mayonnaise. Of course, you can fix a hamburger almost any way you like. As the famous Burger King slogan says, "Have it your way!"

Quiz

Choose the best answer for each question.

1. What was the first chain restaurant in the USA to serve hamburgers?
   A. White Castle   C. McDonald's
   B. Burger King   D. World's Fair

2. Which food is NOT thought of as an American food?
   A. hamburgers   C. hot dogs
   B. popcorn   D. pizza

3. Which sentence is NOT true about hamburgers?
   A. The word "hamburger" comes from German.
   B. Hamburgers have always been the most popular food in America.
   C. The first McDonald's restaurant was in California.
   D. There are many popular fast food hamburgers chains in the USA.

Vocabulary

Use the words in the box to complete the sentences.

popcorn	patty	chain	served
perfected	grill	pickles	ketchup

1. _____ is a thick sauce made from tomatoes and spices.

2. Some people say the first hamburgers were _____ at the 1904 World's Fair in St. Louis.

3. A _____ is a metal frame used for cooking over a fire.

4. McDonald's is probably the most famous fast food _____ in the world.

5. Some people like to put _____ on a hamburger.

6. A hamburger _____ is usually made of ground beef.

7. _____ is actually a very old Native American food.

8. The McDonald brothers _____ the fast food system.

Activity

Eating Habits

Make a questionnaire about eating habits and ask your questions to all the members of your class. Then, make a short report about the findings, or results.

Questionnaire

Write five questions about food that you want to ask your classmates. Try to ask everyone in the class. You may need another paper to record the answers.

	Questions	Answers
1		
2		
3		
4		
5		

Findings

Try to explain your findings like this:

"*About half of the class eats three meals a day.*" OR "*About 50% of the students in the class eat three meals a day.*"

"*6 out of 17 people said they eat rice every day.*" OR "*About one-third of the class eats rice every day.*"

_____

_____

_____

_____

_____

Unit 17: The Grand Canyon

Warm Up

1. Would you prefer to take a vacation in a big city or in nature?

2. What is the most beautiful place you've ever been to?

3. What place would you like to visit in the USA?

Reading

The Grand Canyon

The USA is a large country that covers almost every type of climate and geography. There are beaches and rocky coasts on both the Atlantic Ocean and Pacific Ocean. There are Great Lakes and long rivers. There are small islands and vast open spaces of land. There are forests with the tallest trees in the world, mountains of all sizes, and Great Plains whose farms help to feed the world.

Although people around the world are probably most familiar with American companies and their products, fast food restaurants, movies and music, the USA is also home to some of the most beautiful nature in the world. Much of this nature is protected in the country's national parks.

Every year, hundreds of millions of visitors come to these parks. The five most popular national parks in the USA are: the Great Smoky Mountains, Grand Canyon, Rocky Mountain, Yosemite, and Yellowstone, which was also the world's first national park.

While all these places are unique and beautiful, the Grand Canyon is surely one of the greatest natural wonders in the world. The Grand Canyon—located in Arizona State—is a massive canyon that has been carved out by the Colorado River over millions of years. The Grand Canyon is 277 miles long, 18 miles wide at the widest point, and over a mile deep at various points.

While it is not quite the longest, deepest, or widest canyon in the world, the views from the rim are probably the most spectacular in the world. Millions of tourists—from the USA and abroad—come every year to look at the incredible scenery from many of the lookout spots throughout the park.

In addition to sightseeing from the rim, many visitors enjoy hiking, camping, rafting, and helicopter rides. Because the canyon is so big, it is very difficult to hike down to the river and back up to the rim in one day. You must be in excellent shape, have good weather, and have the right clothes, shoes, and supplies. Every year, park rangers have to rescue people who hike down but can't make it back up. So, if you visit Grand Canyon National Park, please enjoy the views, but be careful.

Quiz

Choose the best answer for each question.

1. What is the oldest national park in the world?
    A. Yellowstone
    C. Grand Canyon
    B. Yosemite
    D. Great Smoky Mountains

2. Which activity is NOT popular at the Grand Canyon?
    A. hiking
    C. sightseeing
    B. swimming
    D. helicopter rides

3. What is probably the most spectacular thing about the Grand Canyon?
    A. It is the longest, widest, and deepest canyon in the world.
    B. It gets more visitors than any other national park.
    C. Hiking from the rim to the bottom of the canyon is enjoyable.
    D. The views from the rim are really impressive.

Vocabulary

Use the words in the box to complete the sentences.

canyon	geography	vast	massive
plains	spectacular	scenery	rescue

1. A _____ is a deep valley, usually with rock walls and a river in it.

2. Every year, park rangers have to _____ people who are lost or hurt.

3. The _____ from the rim of the canyon is spectacular.

4. If something is _____, it is very, very big.

5. _____ is similar to massive, but it is often used to describe places that are wide and/or extend for a long distance.

6. Did you study _____ in junior high school?

7. What is the most _____ sight you've ever seen?

8. The middle of the USA is covered with vast _____.

Activity

The Great Outdoors

Look at these sets of words. Each number has four words, but one of the words in each set may NOT match the others.
Cross out the word that you think does NOT belong in each set. Explain why it doesn't match the other three words. Different answers are possible.

1.	hiking	camping	rafting	skiing
2.	mountain	valley	hill	peak
3.	massive	vast	huge	tiny
4.	tree	bush	plant	rock
5.	incredible	ordinary	amazing	remarkable
6.	surfing	sledding	skiing	ice skating
7.	river	stream	canal	creek
8.	plain	stunning	beautiful	gorgeous
9.	snow	rain	hail	fog
10.	tent	raft	canoe	kayak
11.	mouse	bee	spider	butterfly
12.	lion	fox	coyote	wolf
13.	deer	moose	buffalo	horse
14.	cat	beaver	squirrel	rabbit
15.	sun	moon	planet	sky

Unit 18: Silicon Valley

Warm Up

1. Do you know who the two men in the photo are?

2. What companies did these two men start?

3. What kind of electronic devices do you use?

Reading

Silicon Valley

Can you imagine a world without personal computers, smartphones, and the Internet? For most people in the USA, these things are such a big part of daily life that it seems hard to imagine living without them. But it wasn't really that long ago that all of these things did not exist.

Modern computers have been around since the 1940s, but those early computers were huge machines that filled entire offices. No one had a computer in their home until the development of integrated circuits (or microchips) became widely available in the late 1970s and early 1980s. These microchips were usually made of silicon. When many new companies began manufacturing microchips and other computer equipment in the San Jose region of Northern California, the area became known as "Silicon Valley."

Today, Silicon Valley is home to many of the world's largest high-tech companies, as well as thousands of chip manufacturers, research facilities, and "startup" companies. Apple, Google, Facebook, Intel, and Yahoo! are just a few of the notable companies whose headquarters are in Silicon Valley.

The two most famous computer companies in the USA are probably Apple and Microsoft. These two companies were founded and led by two of the giants in the history of personal computers—Steve Jobs and Bill Gates.

Bill Gates was a very intelligent young man. He entered Harvard University in 1973. He dropped out and started Microsoft in 1975 with a partner, Paul Allen. He was only 20 years old. Much like Henry Ford had done with the automobile, Gates and Allen recognized the possibility of designing personal computers that were cheap and easy to use. Microsoft's software—notably the Windows operating system—became the dominant OS for personal computers. Bill Gates went on to become the richest person in the world.

Steve Jobs also was a bright young man who dropped out of college. He also had a vision for transforming the computer from a large, complicated, and expensive machine into a tool that ordinary people could use and enjoy. He started Apple in 1976 with co-founder Steve Wozniak. Their first office was in the garage of Steve Jobs's parents' home in Silicon Valley. Apple grew to become the world's largest high-tech company, and their devices have gone on to revolutionize the Internet age.

Quiz

Choose the best answer for each question.

1. Where is Silicon Valley?
   A. Alaska
   C. California
   B. Hawaii
   D. Texas

2. Who is the co-founder of Microsoft?
   A. Bill Gates
   C. Henry Ford
   B. Steve Jobs
   D. Steve Wozniak

3. What do Steve Jobs and Bill Gates have in common?
   A. They both went to Harvard University.
   B. They both transformed microchips from germanium into silicon.
   C. They both founded highly successful companies in the 1970s.
   D. They both worked for Google in Silicon Valley.

Vocabulary

Use the words in the box to complete the sentences.

microchip	smartphone	equipment	startup
silicon	software	revolutionize	complicated

1. A _____ is a very small and important part of a computer.
2. Most microchips are made of _____.
3. The iPhone, made by Apple, is a very popular _____.
4. A lot of computer _____ is manufactured in Silicon Valley.
5. Bill Gates is sometimes called the "King of _____."
6. Steve Jobs wanted to _____, or completely change, the way people used personal computers.
7. A _____ company is a new business, often one that needs financial help to get started.
8. The first computers were very _____; they were not easy to use.

Activity

Name Brand Power

Companies like Apple and Microsoft have very strong brand names. Most people recognize and respect products made by these companies. What are some other companies, products, or services with very powerful brand names?

Talk about it with your classmates. Make a list of "powerful brands."

Next, listen to your teacher. Write the names of the companies you hear. Did you name some of the same companies?

My List of Powerful Brands	Top Global Brands
	1.
	2.
	3.
	4.
	5.
	6.
	7.
	8.
	9.
	10.
	11.
	12.

Unit 19: American Holidays

Warm Up

1. How many American holidays can you name?

2. Are any of those days also holidays in your country?

3. What's your favorite holiday? Why do you like it?

Reading

American Holidays

Americans enjoy celebrating their nation's public holidays, just like people from most countries. But, the USA doesn't have so many public holidays. Today, there are ten federal, or national, holidays in the USA.

In 1870, the first four official federal holidays were established by the US government. They are New Year's Day, Independence Day, Thanksgiving, and Christmas.

George Washington's Birthday (also called Presidents' Day), Decoration Day (now called Memorial Day), and Labor Day were all added in the 19th century. In 1938, Armistice Day (now known as Veterans Day) was added to commemorate the end of World War I.

Columbus Day—the day on which Columbus "discovered" the New World—did not become a federal holiday until 1968. And in 1983, Martin Luther King, Jr. Day was established as the country's newest holiday.

These ten holidays are also state holidays in most states, although there are sometimes small differences. In Texas, for example, Columbus Day is not a state holiday, but Christmas Eve and the day after Christmas are.

There are also many other important days for Americans that are not recognized by the government as official holidays. Many of these days have religious, historical, or cultural significance for some Americans. Some examples of these special days are Mardi Gras, St. Patrick's Day, Cinco de Mayo, Kwanzaa, Valentine's Day, Easter, Halloween, and Hannukah. Because the USA is such a diverse country, there are many special days and celebrations that are important to different groups of Americans.

For a majority of Americans, though, the three most popular holidays are Christmas, Thanksgiving, and Independence Day. Christmas is the most important and widely celebrated holiday in the USA. Christmas is important as both a religious and a secular holiday. For many Americans, Christmas represents the birth of Jesus Christ—a time to remember and celebrate the baby who became the Christian savior. To others, Christmas is a just a happy time to give and receive presents, decorate their homes, and anticipate the arrival of Santa Claus.

Quiz

Choose the best answer for each of the following questions.

1. How many national holidays are there in the USA?
   A. 9   B. 10   C. 11   D. 12

2. Which special day is NOT an official federal holiday?
   A. Christmas B. Easter C. Columbus Day D. Memorial Day

3. What is the newest federal holiday in the USA?
   A. Valentine's Day
   B. New Year's Day
   C. George Washington's Birthday
   D. Martin Luther King, Jr. Day

Vocabulary

Use the words in the box to complete the sentences.

public	federal	commemorate	celebrate
labor	established	religious	secular

1. _____ has the same meaning as central or national.

2. _____ means to keep remembering a special day or event.

3. Even though Columbus arrived in the New World in 1492, the holiday to commemorate his discovery was not _____ until 1968.

4. If something is _____, it does not belong to any one group or individual; it is something that is for all people.

5. Easter and Christmas are important _____ holidays in the USA.

6. A _____ celebration is not religious.

7. How do you usually _____ New Year's Eve?

8. Many countries have a holiday to honor workers, or the _____ force.

Activity

American Holidays and Celebrations

Write the names of the American holidays and celebrations in the chart. Look at the Reading passage or use the Internet to help you.

	Date	Holiday	description
1	January 1		start of the calendar year
2	3rd Monday in Jan.		honors the great civil rights leader who was born on Jan. 15
3	February 14		sweethearts exchange gifts or go on a romantic date
4	3rd Monday in Feb.		commemorates the birthday of the first US President
5	late February		Carnival celebration; literally means "Fat Tuesday"
6	Sunday after spring equinox full moon		celebrates Jesus Christ rising from death; egg decorating
7	last Monday in May		day to remember all the soldiers who died in wars
8	July 4		celebrates the *Declaration of Independence*; fireworks
9	1st Monday in Sept.		recognizes all workers and the role of labor in society
10	2nd Monday in Oct.		commemorates the "discovery" of America
11	October 31		celebrated with trick-or-treating and costume parties
12	November 11		end of World War 1; honors all veterans of the armed forces
13	4th Thursday in Nov.		celebrated by giving thanks for food and life; turkey dinner
14	December 24		Santa Claus delivers presents to boys and girls
15	December 25		commemorates the birth of Jesus Christ
16	December 31		end of the calendar year; countdown parties

*Numbers 3, 5, 6, 11, 14 and 16 are NOT national holidays.

Unit 20: The USA in the 21st Century

Warm Up

1. When were you born? When were your parents born?

2. How is the world different now from 30 years ago?

3. What do you think is the biggest challenge of your generation?

Reading

The USA in the 21st Century

As we read in Unit 10, the 20th century was called the "American Century" because the USA was the leading economic and military power during most of that century. But what about America's role in the 21st century?

Will the USA continue to be a powerful nation? Will other countries replace the USA in terms of economic or military strength? Will the USA still continue to export its culture around the world as it did in the 20th century? We can't answer these questions yet. No one knows what will happen and how the USA might change in the future. Like other nations, the USA faces many challenges in the coming decades.

The 21st century did not begin very well for the USA. On September 11, 2001, one of the greatest tragedies in American history took place. Terrorists attacked the twin towers of the World Trade Center in New York City with hijacked airliners. The towers were destroyed and thousands of people were killed.

In the years following this shocking attack, Americans seemed to become more fearful of the world around them and perhaps less welcoming toward people from other countries. Under President George W. Bush, the US government launched the "War on Terror" in Afghanistan and Iraq. New laws and agencies were created to protect the country from terrorism. Security at airports was tightened, and immigration became more difficult.

In 2008, Barack Obama became the first African American president in US history. His positive message "Yes, We Can!" offered hope to minority groups. Obama began a public health insurance program for all Americans, and the US economy came back very strong after the world financial crisis.

Donald Trump was elected the 45th President of the USA in a very bitter and controversial election in 2016. Promising to "Make America Great Again", his ideas and programs were often directly the opposite of those America had experienced during eight years under Obama. Trump is certainly one of the most unique and controversial presidents in US history. Many people now feel that the USA is more divided than ever.

There are plenty of challenges in the years ahead. How will countries balance globalization with protecting their own interests and culture? What about global warming? And the growing income gap between rich and poor? Can Americans overcome the political, racial, and religious differences that have often divided them? Only time will tell.

Quiz

Choose the best answer for each question.

1. What happened on September 11, 2001?
   A. The US government launched the "War on Terror."
   B. Terrorists attacked the World Trade Center towers with hijacked airliners.
   C. Millions of Americans were killed by terrorism.
   D. New York City was attacked by Iraq and Afghanistan.

2. Who was the first black person to become president of the United States?
   A. Donald Trump
   B. Barack Obama
   C. Martin Luther King, Jr.
   D. George Washington

3. What will the role of the USA be like in the 21st century?
   A. The War on Terror will be led by the US armed forces.
   B. The USA will continue to have the world's strongest economy.
   C. The USA will overcome its racial and religious prejudices.
   D. No one really knows how the role of the USA will change in this century.

Vocabulary

Use the words in the box to complete the sentences.

century	tragedy	challenges	military
terrorism	security	divided	election

1. A _____ is a very bad event or situation.
2. Like other countries, the USA will face many _____ this century.
3. After 9-11 (September 11, 2001), airport _____ was tightened.
4. The US government focused on fighting _____ after 9-11.
5. A _____ is a time period of 100 years.
6. _____ means the opposite of united.
7. Donald Trump won a bitter and controversial _____ in 2016.
8. Most Americans think it's important to have a strong _____.

Activity

Comparing Cultures

Review the information you learned about the USA in this class. Then, add information about your own country. Discuss the differences, or write a report explaining the biggest differences between the USA and your country.

	USA	my country
Geography		
Climate		
Cities		
History		
Population		
Race & Ethnicity		
Government		
Economy & Industry		
Food		
Holidays		
Language		
Future Challenges		

Facts about the U.S.A.

Flag:    **Great Seal:**

Motto: "In God We Trust" (official)   *"E pluribus unum"* (traditional)

National Anthem: *The Star-Spangled Banner*

Capital: Washington, D.C.

Independence Day: July 4, 1776

Area: 9,826,675 sq. km.   *3rd largest country by size (after Russia and Canada)*

Largest State (size):   Alaska   **Smallest State:**   Rhode Island

Population: 320,000,000 (2015 estimate)   *3rd largest country by population (after China and India)*

Largest Cities (population):   New York, Los Angeles, Chicago, Houston, Philadelphia, Phoenix, San Antonio, San Diego, Dallas, San Jose

Bordering Countries: Canada, Mexico

Highest point: Mt. McKinley, Alaska (6,194 meters above sea level)

Lowest point: Death Valley, California (86 meters below sea level)

Government: Federal presidential constitutional republic

President: 45th President: Donald Trump   (elected 2016)

Chief Justice: John Roberts   (appointed 2005)

Legislature: Congress comprised of Senate and House of Representatives

Race/Ethnic groups: White (non-Hispanic) 62%, Hispanic 16%, Black 13%, Asian and Pacific Islander 6%, Native American %1, other %2   (2014 estimates)

Languages: English 82%, Spanish 11%, other Indo-European 4%, Asian and Pacific Islands 3%, other 1%   (2010 census)

Religions: Protestant 52%, Roman Catholic 24%, Mormon 2%, Jewish 1%, Muslim 1%, other 10%, none 10%

Currency: US dollar

Coins: 1¢ = penny, 5¢ = nickel, 10¢ = dime, 25¢ = quarter, $1.00 = silver dollar

GDP (PPP):   Total: $15.685 trillion   *(world's largest)*

Per capita: $49,922   *(world's 6th highest country)*   (2014 estimates)

U.S. Postal Codes

These are the official 2-letter state codes used by the US Postal Service.

AL		MT	
AK		NE	
AZ		NV	
AR		NH	
CA		NJ	
CO		NM	
CT		NY	
DE		NC	
FL		ND	
GA		OH	
HI		OK	
ID		OR	
IL		PA	
IN		RI	
IA		SC	
KS		SD	
KY		TN	
LA		TX	
ME		UT	
MD		VT	
MA		VA	
MI		WA	
MN		WV	
MS		WI	
MO		WY	

Additional 2-letter postal codes for other parts (non-states) of the USA.

DC		PR	
AS		VI	
GU			

63810606R00051

Made in the USA
Middletown, DE
06 February 2018